Pr

Danger

Pre-Packed Danger

James Meadows

Paper Doll

© James Meadows 1998

Published by Paper Doll
Belasis Hall
Coxwold Way
Billingham
Cleveland

ISBN: 1 86248 053 2

Typeset by CBS, Felixstowe, Suffolk
Printed by Lintons Printers, Co. Durham

CONTENTS

PRE-PACKED DANGER

Why is it that everything we buy
From socks and shirt to coloured tie,
From screws and hooks to white elastic
Must be packed in rock hard plastic?

Plastic now plays a large part in our lives
When seeking presents for girlfriends and wives
The items we purchase their glories reveal
In a transparent pack with unbreakable seal.

Look all around and what do you see?
If it isn't the one then it's PVC.
From door handles, locks and rainwater chutes
To luminous 'macs' and ankle length boots.

This material supplies our everyday needs,
But beware of complacency, listen, take heed.
It has hidden power which man does not know
And is gathering strength for one final blow.

When it makes its attack on our civilisation
We shall one day awake to the realisation
That we are in packets, plastic festooned,
Captured for ever, marooned and cocooned.

LEGALISED RAPE

It took twenty thousand acres of good land.
Enough to provide food for a small country for a
 year.
It compulsorily purchased the homes of
Eleven hundred sparrows, fifty blackbirds,
Twenty foxes, twelve hundred rabbits,
Countless mice, butterflies and moths, and
Although it misses the church steeple,
No work remained for a hundred people.
Pleasant lanes were blocked up, widened,
Narrowed, raised, lowered, realigned and spanned
By cold grey concrete bridges for all to see
This impersonal, tarmacadamed monster in all
 its
Dual carriage-wayed, three-laned, safety-factored
 glory,
Cutting hours off the journey from A to B.
So now we can get there in half the time
It took on the old, dangerous, winding roads.
But gone are the pleasures of travel and
The delights of the shady lay-by on the A 49.
Through cutting, embankment, flyover and
 underpass,
Runs this monument to our four-wheeled god,
Built by modern technology and the sweat of
 itinerant labourers.
It has eaten our land, the source of our food,
Left scars no landscape artist can ever improve.
Put a blight on our hunting, shooting and courting,

And what does it give for our money supporting
Its conception, birth and permanent nurture?
What return, interest or hope for the future?

Nothing more than the right to drive at 70 miles
    per hour
Through nowhere to our certain end.

IF

If I had a yacht, love,
We could sail the seas.
If I had ten servants, love,
You could take your ease.
If I had a plane, love,
We could fly away.
If I owned a golf club
Just you and I could play.
If I had no wife, love,
You and I could wed
But I only have this urge, love,
So let's go to bed.

BUT

But you have no yacht, sir,
So there'll be no cruise.
You can't afford the servants
For me to pick and choose.
But you have no plane, sir,
To soar up in the air.
But you have no golf club
Where we could make a pair.
But you have a wife, sir,
To whom your love is due.
And to tell the truth, sir,
I could never fancy you.

DREAMS

I waited for you
Once again last night
To join me
In the dream world
That is ours alone.
But you did not come.
Locked in my mind
My love for you
Sustains my waking hours.
But once asleep
The loneliness begins.
Do not desert me
When I need you most.

IMAGINATION

Iron horse charging down the rails,
Moaning wind, rain's piercing nails,
Apparitions in the clouds,
Ghostly figures, empty shrouds.
Icy roads resembling glass,
Nodding flowers in the grass.
Acrobatic birds in flight,
Twinkling jewels of starlight.
Inscribe such sights within your memory,
Now imagination's imagery.

SOUNDS OF THE ANIMAL KINGDOM

Adventurous apes advancing round the cage,
Lugubrious lions lunging in mock rage.
Lurking lynx looking for its prey,
Immobile iguana indented in the clay.
Terrible tiger turning round and round,
Elegant elephant emitting great sound.
Revolting rhinoceros rumbling here and there,
Armoured armadillo averting people's stare.
Trembling tortoise turning in its shell,
Imperial ibis imposing its spell.
Some animals of every nation
Not only that but you've got alliteration.

DOORSTEP DUET

Knock, knock!
I've called for the rent.
    It's spent.
But you must pay.
    I can't today
    Nor tomorrow.

But a lot depends
On paying what's due
Or you
Will find yourself convicted
And evicted
From your home.

    Home you say,
    Go to hell!
    You know damned well
    The roof leaks
    The stairs creak.
    There's a hole in the door
    And rot in the floor
    There's not a screw
    In the door to the loo.

    It's damp and cold as the grave.
    You heartless knave
    Asking for rent
    For a place like this.

Pay the rent.
That's a joke.
You can poke
Your hand through the wall
And that's not all.

There's rats and mice
Woodworm and lice
Under the floors
And in the doors
I won't pay.
The money I'll use
For fags and booze.
And to feed my ten kids.

But you must cope
You haven't a hope
Of staying here
If you spend on beer
What is due
To the landlord from you.
So pay me now
And avoid a row.
For unless it's paid
I shall be made
To apply to the court
And get you out.

Please give me time.
Besides you
There's the man from the Pru,
The fridge and the telly,
Four mail order clubs,
Christmas club subs.
The corner shop,
Coal from the Co-op.
And a lot more to be paid.

It must be today!
Oh what can I say?
I could pay in kind.

Well I don't mind.
Just step inside
And I will provide
You with pleasures sublime.
Hang your coat on the door
And you shall explore
Areas of joy
Only dreamt of before.
(George now be quick
And you can nick
What he's collected today)

He lost all his rents
Because he went
Into forbidden ground.
He'd have been given the sack
And made to pay back

That considerable treasure
As the price of his pleasure.
The wages of sin
Would have been heaped upon him.

BUT

He escaped from it all
With a neck breaking fall.
When
The bed fell through the rotten floor.

SCHOOL SEX LESSON
(WITH APOLOGIES TO HENRY REED)

Today we have naming of parts. Yesterday
We had personal hygiene. And tomorrow morning
We shall have what to do after firing. But today,
Today we have naming of parts. Temptation
Shines like a beacon in all the Perfumed Gardens.
And today we have naming of parts.

These are the upper erogenous zones, and this
Is the lower erogenous zone, the use of which
    you will see
When your instruction is complete. Leading to
    the inner peace
Which in your case you have not got. The
    fantasies
Writhe in the gardens with silent eloquent
    gestures.
Which in our case is all we have got.

This is the breach opening, which is always
    released
With an easy flick of the finger. And please do
    not let me
See anyone using his thumb. You can do it quite
    easily
If you have any strength in your finger. The figures
Are silent and motionless, never letting anyone
    see
Any of them using their thumb.

And this you can see is the phallus. The purpose
     of this
Is to open the breach, as you can see. You slide it
Rapidly backwards and forwards; we call this
Easing the tension. And rapidly backwards and
     forwards
The birds and bees fly from our fumbling minds
Now that we can ease our spring.

Now we can ease our spring. It is perfectly easy
If you have the fire in your loins; with the phallus
And the breach and the driving force, and the
     sense of balance,
Which in our case we have not yet got.
'Till then the inner peace lies hidden in the garden
     with the
Uncoiled spring going backwards and forwards.
But now, at least we can name the parts.

AND AFTERWARDS

Yesterday we were told the names of the parts.
Today we hoped to learn how to use them,
But it did not happen.
All our questions fell on deaf ears.
Leaving us like half trained soldiers, not knowing
How to use what we've been given.
The function of a teacher is to teach.
They tell us how to use our feet, to run, kick
    balls.
Our minds to soak up knowledge for future use.
Our hands to write, to fashion things.
But now it seems we must be kept away
From the parts whose names we know.

We are urged to use the knowledge we have
    gained,
To remember dates, verbs, reasons and results.
To question if we do not understand, to see that
For every action there is a corresponding
    reaction.
But here it seems the rules have changed.
Is there no examination in sex?
So we must keep this knowledge locked away
Until someone tells us how to put it to good use.
Or seek instruction from books and magazines
They would confiscate. Our peers may boast
That they are experts in this field, but then
Like fishermen their catches may be lies.
But at least we can name the parts.

THE HUNT BALL

Four hundred jolly people
Within the castle wall,
Singing and a-dancing
At the annual Hunt Ball.

The noise of celebrations
Blasted o'er the castle keep.
People in the area
Tried in vain to get to sleep.

There were all the county gentry
With wives and ladies too,
Each had paid a princely sum
To dance the whole night through.

The band were dressed in hunting pink
They were a pretty sight.
The dancers cantered round the floor.
Scarce knowing left from right.

They danced around the great hall
And up and down the stairs,
It was hard to find a haven
From the madly prancing pairs.

But as the hour of midnight
Chimed from the castle clocks
There crept into the courtyard
A majestic looking fox.

He ran across the cobbles
And through the open door.
Then slipped between the dancing legs
To the centre of the floor.

The band tailed off in mid note,
The dancers held their breath,
And silence spread around the hall
Like a wave of sudden death.

The fox glanced slowly round him
With a look of quiet disdain,
Then he walked up to the Master
Who was tugging at the rein.

'You have done your best to kill me
The hunting season through.
But now I'm going to take great joy
In my revenge on you.

'In return for all the sport
You've had in chasing me
My friends and I will have this night
A very merry spree.

'Your hounds are safely kennelled
Many miles from here.
You're powerless without their help
We have no cause to fear.

'So tell your guests to leave the hall
And collect up all their coats.
For within these castle walls tonight
They will not get their oats.

'And whilst we eat up all the food
In the courtyard you can wait,
You cannot any farther go
For we have barred the gate.

'You cannot hope to summon help
We've cut the telephone wires,
And to stop you bolting in your cars
We've chewed holes in the tyres.'

The Master stood there speechless
His face as black as coal.
Women screamed slowly floorwards
As if about to foal.

It soon became apparent
That Reynard was in command,
So the couples shuffled from the hall
Behind the dirging band.

For over ninety minutes
They were in the cold night air
Whilst the fox and his companions
Ate up the party fare.

And when the plates were empty
He stood on the topmost step,
And surveyed the silent dancers
Who now began to sweat.

'And now to conclude the evening
We intend to have some fun.
As we chase you o'er the countryside
You for your lives can run.'

The castle gates were opened
And at once the chase began,
As from the snarling foxes
The frightened dancers ran.

Without benefit of horses
The people stood no chance,
And soon the snapping foxes' teeth
Produced a different dance.

They chased them over hedges
They chased them down the lanes,
Despite their size, the people
Sought refuge in the drains.

The chase went on for hours
Through tearing thorns and crags,
The suits and evening dresses
Were soon reduced to rags.

Five hundred tired people
Crawling home all tattered and torn,
Never again will they respond
To the call of the hunting horn.

THE LOTTERY

I am the body
In the hearse you see,
I am the fisherman
Drowned at sea.

I am the victim
Of the aeroplane crash,
I am the pieces
Of a motorway smash.

I am the shoplifter
Paying my fine,
I am the soldier
Killed by a mine.

I am the young girl
Pregnant but single,
I take the drugs
Which make my veins tingle.

I am the drop out
With nothing to give,
I have a family
But nowhere to live.

I am the blind man
The deaf and the dumb,
I am disabled
Rejected by some.

I'm HIV positive
On borrowed time,
I'm the alcoholic
Reduced to cheap wine.

I am the vandal
Wrecking a station,
I am alone
And seeking salvation.

In the lottery of life
This number I drew,
But for the grace of God
I am you.

SHORT SONG OF EXPERIENCE

You are forced to break the habit of a lifetime.
Turning back to collect a forgotten handkerchief
Or to implant one final barb in the fine
Flow of insults to a warring spouse.
Because of this, self activated perhaps,
It's well past eight fifteen when you leave the
house.

Five minutes late, the first time ever,
You hurry, half run, on your way to the stop.
A passing ambulance gives speed to your step,
Perhaps if you hurry there may still be time.
At last you reach the corner to find
Blue lights illuminating twisted metal and human
remains.

A lorry has mown down the waiting queue.
Erasing the expressions from those faces made
familiar
By half obscurity behind the daily papers,
Sometime emerging to condemn the weather.
And you, because you turned back
Are left to wonder and pick up the pieces.

THE BIRTHDAY PRESENT

What can I give to a man
Whose birthday is drawing near?
A man who is always offering things
But I never seem to hear.

Perhaps a year's subscription
To a club to drink and dine,
But would this really impress someone
Who turned water into wine?

I could give a course of instruction
On how to water-ski,
But he showed how many years ago
He could control the sea.

I could give a specially packed hamper
From a fashionable London store,
But to a man who once shunned even bread
Exotic food is a bore.

Shall I give a wristwatch
Jewelled in a golden case?
But perhaps after two thousand years of life
Time of day has little place.

I could give him a new suit
Styled in the latest mode,
But in all the pictures I've seen of him
He only wears a robe.

I could give him the right to live
In any house in the land,
After so many years on the waiting list
Such a gift would be grand.

If I do not make a decision
His gift will stay on the shelf,
Perhaps the best thing I can do
Is just to offer myself.

THE RACE

The Commentator

They thunder up to the water
With Gay Trip in the lead,
The first five are safely over
But a faller is Broken Reed.

Approaching the third fence from home now
The field spread over the course,
The leaders will jump it together
But they're hampered by a loose horse.

The Horses

Why when we lose our riders
Should we also lose our name?
Our numbers are still on our saddles,
Surely we look the same?
(You may be the only grey in the race
But unseat your rider and of course
You become a loose horse).
Is it because riderless we cannot win?
In human terms do you lose your name
When although you look and feel the same
You are no longer able to win the race?

NO ROOM IN THE BIN

We live in a disposable age.
Disposable
Napkins and knickers,
Sheets and shirts,
Bottles and cans.

Progress builds obsolescence
Into
Computers and cameras,
Buildings and boats,
Cars and 'planes.

Will there be room on the tip
For the obsolete,
Disposable, men and women?

WAR IN OUR VILLAGE

After the third of September came the men
With dragon like torches to cut low
The gates and fences which had barred
Our entry to fields and gardens of mystery.
But once the barriers had gone we didn't want to
    know.

After the third of September we carried
Gas masks in boxes of cardboard and wood,
And smelly rubber ear plugs, never used
Except as substitutes for pencil rubbers.
Like the country, we used whatever we could.

After the third of September we prepared
To receive evacuees into our homes and rural
    domain
The air raids had made their towns unsafe,
But despite our efforts they never came
Some official lost their papers and their train.

After the third of September we collected
Waste paper; salvaged all we were able.
With sacks and barrows from house to house
We went, then took it to the collecting place
    where
For years it rotted and smelt in the Vicarage
    stable.

After the third of September soldiers came
With tin cans and evil burning oil
To send up smokescreens to black out
The view from enemy planes whose bombs
Our rural peace, and the local airfield, may
    despoil.

After the third of September, for many years
We collected for battleships and wings,
Dug for victory and robbed the birds
Of every available rose hip for miles.
Besieged visiting American soldiers
'Got any gum, chum?'
Had countless propaganda films
From the Army Kinema Corporation
And the Ministry of Information.
Until one day the world was set free
And the Manor House lawn
Was thrown open for tea.

WE ARE THE CHILDREN

We are the children,
Please give us a chance,
Don't let the politicians
Lead us such a dance.

We are the children,
Through us the world will grow,
Don't let us face this prospect
In misery and woe.

We are the children,
For us a new day breaks,
Let it not be clouded
By previous mistakes.

We are the children,
Give us time to learn,
Don't always look for spending
To have a quick return.

We are the children,
Give us what we need,
For the growth of generations
You must have us, the seed.

We are the children,
The future's in our hands.
Speak to those who rule us,
Make them understand.

We are the children,
Listen to our plea,
From the chains of prejudice
Please may we be free.

We are the children,
Please give us a chance,
Don't let the politicians
Lead us such a dance.

THE GENERAL'S LAMENT

Television has killed the art of war.
How can you use the right tactics if before
You have left the Mess at base
Some nosy camera crew is
Sending back pictures to bridge the space
To the people you are fighting for?

Gone are the days of the glorious battle.
Who would support the heartening rattle
Of sabre, sword and shield
In the Valley of Death if they could see
The whole thing live as it happened
On coloured screen by the BBC?

Gone are the days when we could
Say what we thought they should
Know. Now with improved communications
They can protest and stage demonstrations
To say war is wrong. Curse the day when
They were shown that war matters to them.

NURSERY RHYMES OF OUR TIMES 1

They're changing the guard
On the body of Alice
Who was done to death
Outside the palace.
And while her relatives
Are seen to be sobbing,
The police are searching
For Christopher Robin.

Mary had a flock of lambs,
They could hardly hobble,
For the field that they were grazing
Was rained on from Chernobyl.

Jack and Jill went up the hill
In search of H_2O,
What happened there to make him fall
We shall never know.

INGRATITUDE

I have supported you for years
Through thick and thin,
I've allowed myself to be
Adjusted to your slightest whim.

When you were low I sagged
To blackest depth,
When you were high
I rose with every breath.

I have protected you yet
Stayed behind the scene,
My help was obvious
Yet I remained unseen.

I've held you close
And felt your young heart beat,
I've done my best
To make your life complete.

I have protected you against
All manner of attack,
At all times my defence
Was at your back.

Now in return for all
The years of dedication,
Am I to be cast into
The fires of liberation?

What a way to treat a bra.

WHO IS TO BLAME?

'You're doing my head in
Get off my back.
I hate your lessons,
School is crap.
Shout at me and
You'll get the sack.
I have my rights
You can't touch me.
Extra work, detention,
My Mum will complain,
Just you see
I can do what I like,
So get stuffed
Take a hike.
I don't care
About you or this school.
I don't want to learn
Or stick to the rule.
Report me, send me home,
At least then
I'd not hear you moan.
You could then help the boffins
The fools who want to learn,
Those who haven't seen through you
Who don't your "wisdom" spurn.
Let them examine this problem
An accurate answer to find,
How is it you have managed
To totally poison my mind?'

THOUGHTS FOR THE JOURNEY

'Penalty for improper use of this cord £25'

When can you pull the cord
And be found to be proper
And not be chased
By a railway copper
Demanding his £25?

As your train glides along
The endless track
And you gaze at the notice
At the side of the rack,
As you sweep under a bridge
With a noise like thunder,
Have you ever stopped to wonder
What is a proper use?

If you've left your teeth
In a station pork pie,
Or have pains in your chest
And feel you will die.
If you're locked in the loo
And the door is stuck fast
You then start to worry
Your station's been passed.
If you awake from a dream
Of impending disaster
And your whole body quivers
As the train goes faster.

If you drop a live match
On your travelling cape
Or are locked in a carriage
With a man bent on rape,
If you can't find your ticket
As the inspector approaches,
Or realise for your station
It's the first three coaches.

Would you then pull the cord
Knowing you could not afford
To pay the twenty-five poundssss?

WAR OF THE WORDS

'Listen to me,'
Roared the noun.
'I am king of the words,
You really must own
Without me
There'd be no name,
All the things in the world
Would be called the same.
Roses, raspberries,
Head and heart
Never could be
Told apart.'

The mild mannered adjective
Rose to speak.
'It may seem to you
That I am quite weak.
Although I do not
Wish to be rude
Without my help
You're totally nude.
Only I can tell
If you're black or white
Fat, tall, thin,
Wrong or right.'

Into the fray
Then came the verb.
'This argument

Is quite absurd.
A plague I say
On all your factions
For I am the basis
Of all actions.
If you would rave,
Posture or shout
You'll always need me
To help you out.'

The adverb rapidly
Came to life.
'Although I'm reluctant
To add to this strife
I can't leave unanswered
Verb's tirade,
He counts for little
Without my aid.
He leaves his actions
Floating in air.
Men wish to know
How, when, why or where.'

Others then stated
Their position,
A determiner punched
A preposition.
Conjunction tried hard
To unite friend and foe,
Pronoun told noun
In his place he would go.

So the battle raged
With various interjections,
O how silly are these words
To form such rigid sections.

They all have
A part to play
In our life and thoughts
In what we write and say.
If you use them wisely
There is no need to stress
The problems you encounter
If you use them to excess.
Do not use too many words
To make your meaning clear,
Or the reader may decide
You have verbal diarrhoea.

NURSERY RHYMES OF OUR TIMES 2

Humpty Dumpty sat on the wall
What a silly fellow,
If he should fall and break
We'll all get salmonella.

Little Miss Muffet
Sat on a tuffet
Towards the end of the day,
But it wasn't a spider
Who sat down beside her
And had his wicked way.

VALENTINES

Poets write sonnets
Song writers praise bonnets,
To show the strength of their love.
But what can I do to melt
The heart of iron
In the body of a dove?

This Valentine is sent to you
You'll probably not get another,
I sent it out of charity.
My identity? Just don't bother.

People say that love is blind,
It ignores all imperfections,
If that's the case
Then why the hell
Have I had so many rejections?

The moon enhances your beauty
Candles your features display,
If only you weren't so ugly
In the cold, clear light of day.

WELSH BEACHES 1950

Who would think when seeing
Your twice daily washed and ironed glory
On a clear winter's day,
Smooth and unmarked save for
The claws of gliding gulls,
That within a few short months
You will be colonised
By thousands of colliers and steel workers,
Civil servants and clerks.
On day trips from Newport, Caldicott,
Bargoed, Bedlinog and Splott.
They will turn your surface into
Countless castles, moats and tunnels;
Erect screens to keep out winds
And prying chapel eyes.
Put up deck chairs, litter food,
Then complain of flies.
Turn you for a few brief moments
Into Wembley, Lords, the Arms Park,
Living out their fantasies.
When darkness falls they leave you
With ice cream papers, cans,
Half eaten sandwiches and lost shoes
To be swept up by your ebbing tide.
Briefly your winter's peace returns.
Disturbed only by the glare and blaze
Of throbbing dance halls.
Now is the time to rest, O sands,
Accommodate intrepid lovers in your hands,

Tomorrow and tomorrow brings a fresh assault,
Until the earth turns far enough
To give you seasonal rest.

INFANT WELFARE

I give thanks to the state
Lying here in my cushioned home,
Protected by a wall of legislation,
For once I am born
I know the state will
Immunise and orange juice me,
Weigh and measure me.
And through its army of
Health visitors and social workers,
Doctors and Dentists,
Clinics and nurseries,
Begin to claim me
For its own.

Then I can be
Educated and instructed,
Tuned and trained,
Tidied and turned
Into a model citizen.
Fit to take my place
In the scheme of life.
Until I am worn out
And then the state
Will pension and protect me
And even bury me
When I die.

If I should return
When this life is done
Let it be as a bird
And then I can be free.

ACADEMIC RACE

With the strength of ten GCSEs
A reasonable path you can choose,
It should be enough to get ahead
Of those with N.V.Q.s.

Diplomas and degrees with honours
Will many people please,
But they may be overtaken
By Masters and PhDs.

But what of the outsiders
Who cannot such form exhibit,
Should they think lack of training
Their progress will inhibit?

Although to the obvious favourites
They may not quite compare,
They can take some comfort
From the tortoise and the hare.

COLOURS

When in my teens
Each day was blue
Of cheerful kind
No morbid hue.
Now
Each morning brings
Another red letter day,
Gas, rates, electricity,
Demands to pay.

THE XENOPHOBIC ALPHABET

Australians curse in the sun.
Belgians seldom have much fun.
Canadians are a race most dour
Danes cream cakes and bacon devour.
Egyptians live in the sands.
Frenchmen talk with their hands.
Germans accept hard work and play
Hungarians used to dance all day.
Indians wear clothes most floppy
Japanese search for things to copy.
Kenyans exploit their game park
Laplanders spend half the year in the dark.
Mexicans under large hats sleep
New Zealanders are outnumbered by sheep.
Orientals have great mystery
Poles struggle with their history.
Quatarians get rich from oil
Russians are always in turmoil.
Spaniards still bulls fight.
Turks glory in delight.
Ukrainians suffer hard times
Venezuelans make money from mines.
Welshmen live for games and singing
Xenophobes these words no friends are winning.
You'll be isolated if you
Zealously believe them to be true.

LOOKING AND SEARCHING

Rejoice in the beauty of nature,
Birds, flowers, plants and trees,
All given to us with
The power to see,
But not believed
'Till artificially produced
In photographs.

Rejoice in the power of the earth,
Sun, wind, rain and snow
With its secret bleaching ingredient.
Always with us but taken for granted
Until they show their strength
By melting roads or flooding the earth
With a downpour preceded by
Wind, lightning
And ear splitting celestial percussion.

We see but must be made to believe.
We hear but fail to comprehend.
We search for signs we shall not understand.
Should we struggle on like Pilgrim
Or like Shaw's Black Girl take Bible as a route
    map?
Can we 'phone for help when lost or diverted?
There are no motorways where we are going
Even if we knew the way.

SHAPES OF WAR

War
Took away
Fathers from families
Few of whom
Knew what they
Were fighting
For.

State
Before self
Was the cry,
Now we are free.
But for them
It's too
Late.

Glance
At the monuments
Telling us
'They shall grow not old',
They never had
The bloody
Chance.

WIDOW'S EASTER HYMN

On this day we rejoice that death
Can no longer hurt us with its sting.
By His rising we are told this is so,
But can I believe it with a husband
In a field of clay I do not know?

If He could beat death then surely
He could have stopped this war
Which has stolen the man in my life.
I have always tried to be good.
Why should I be widow and not wife?

Soon the children will return from church,
Full of joy from the Easter service.
They still believe He shows the way,
But how long will they keep their faith
Knowing their father died for ever
This Easter Day?

CHILDREN'S PRAYER

Bless our Mummy, make her strong
To make up for Daddy, who died fighting wrong.

Bless our house and please, please keep
Us safe from air raids whilst we sleep.

Bless the people who made Daddy fight
In a war which they must think is right.

Bless our country that it may win
The war it is fighting to overcome sin.

Bless us both and please help us see
Why our Daddy died for the world to be free.

Please why did You let it happen?

PUNCTUATION

I am a jolly full stop
Sitting on the line.
Splitting up the sentences
Letting people breath,
Making sure your writing
Can proper sense achieve.

I wish I were a comma
Building up a list,
Giving people time to think,
Get tongues out of a twist.
This gentle sort of life
Would really suit me fine,
Keeping all the words apart
As I lie here on the line.

Gosh! Golly!
Listen! Hark!
I am a jolly
Exclamation mark.
Standing upright on the line
Pointing to the ceiling,
Just to make sure that you know
Words are said with feeling.

I am a nosy question mark
Asking who? When? Why? or Where?
Seeking information
Of me you must beware.

I have the curiosity
Of a well trained cat,
And if you do not answer
I'll try with how? or what?

We the inverted commas show
The words which have been spoken.
We live by simple rules
Which never must be broken.
You must keep within our boundaries
Spoken word or quotation
And don't forget to include
All the punctuation.

Spare a thought for the hyphen
Floating in the air.
A little line between two words
Not going anywhere.
It'll never gain much glory,
Never earn much cash.
To most ordinary people
It's nothing but a dash

The semi-colon is a mixture
Of comma and full stop.
The comma lying on the line
The full stop on the top.
It's stronger than the first one
But weaker than the last.
In replacing a conjunction
It can not be outclassed.

The words before a colon make sense
So it may seem to some quite dense
And totally over the top
To use it in place of a full stop.
You should, however stop and reflect,
It can increase dramatic effect.

The apostrophe floats in the air
Showing that letters
Are missing somewhere
It's easy to see that's a vital task
But can it do more
I hear you ask.
Yes, it can show possession,
The man's dilemma
The sinner's confession.
But check the facts,
Don't just guess.
It's not always used
When the word ends in s.